STEP-BY-STEP

MODELS

SARA GRISEWOOD

ILLUSTRATED BY JIM ROBINS

Kingfisher

KINGFISHER
An imprint of Larousse plc
Elsley House,
24-30 Great Titchfield Street,
London W1P 7AD

First published by Kingfisher 1994

10 9 8 7 6 5 4 3 2

A CIP catalogue record for this
book is available from the
British Library

ISBN 1 85697 232 1

Series editor: Deri Robins
Edited by Hazel Poole
Designed by Ben White
Illustrations by Jim Robins
Photographed by Rolf Cornell,
  SCL Photographic Services
Cover design by Terry Woodley
Typeset in 3B2 by
  Tracey McNerney
Phototypeset by SPAN
  (Southern Positives and Negatives),
  Lingfield, Surrey
Printed in Hong Kong

CONTENTS

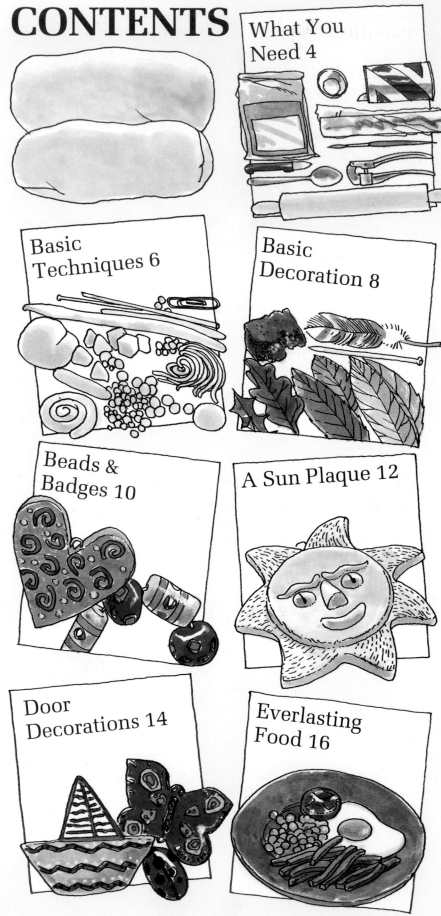

Here you can see some of the basic materials that you'll need to make the models in this book. Before you start to make each model though, read through its instructions to see if you'll need any other special materials.

Modelling 'Clays'

There are several types of modelling 'clays' available, but in this book we'll be using just two – salt-dough and self-hardening clay.

Salt-dough is made from flour and water (see page 6), and is baked in the oven.

Self-hardening clay can be bought from most toy shops and art-and-craft suppliers. Read the instructions on the back of the packet before you start.

Flour

Salt

Self-hardening clay

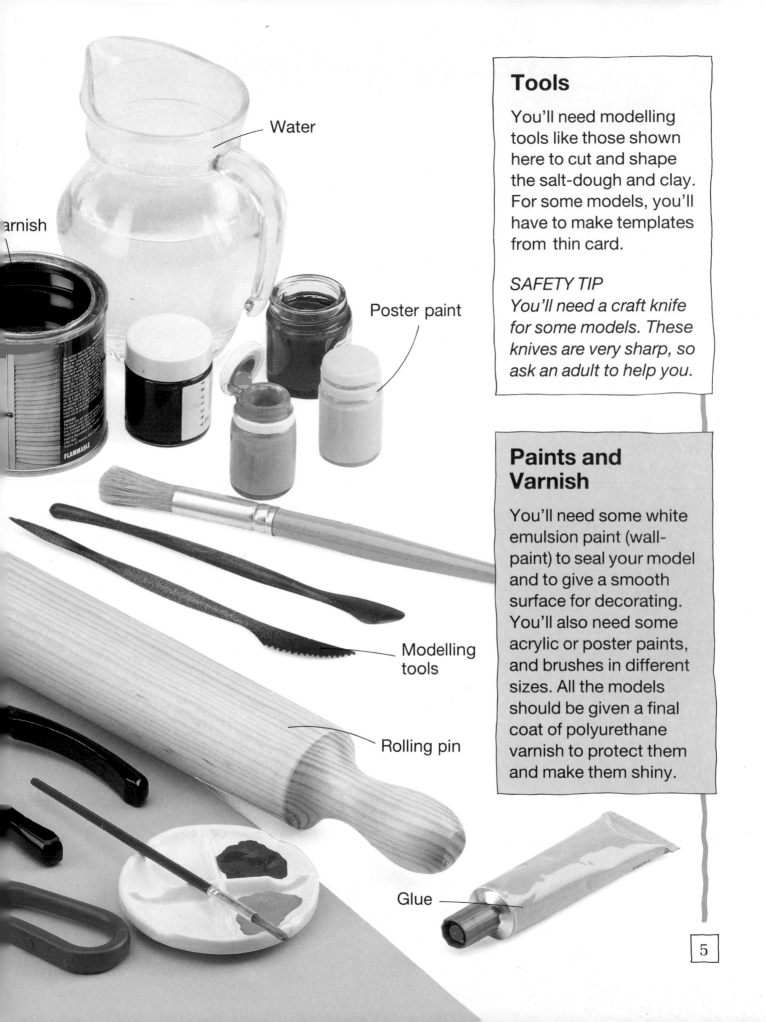

Water

arnish

Poster paint

Modelling
tools

Rolling pin

Glue

Tools

You'll need modelling
tools like those shown
here to cut and shape
the salt-dough and clay.
For some models, you'll
have to make templates
from thin card.

SAFETY TIP
You'll need a craft knife
for some models. These
knives are very sharp, so
ask an adult to help you.

Paints and Varnish

You'll need some white
emulsion paint (wall-
paint) to seal your model
and to give a smooth
surface for decorating.
You'll also need some
acrylic or poster paints,
and brushes in different
sizes. All the models
should be given a final
coat of polyurethane
varnish to protect them
and make them shiny.

BASIC TECHNIQUES

Many of the models in this book are made from salt-dough, which you can make following the recipe below. Both this and self-hardening clay are easy to work with – so have fun!

Making Dough

Mix together 100 grams salt with 340 grams plain flour in a mixing bowl. Slowly add 225-350 ml lukewarm water, and mix together until you have a soft dough. Knead the dough for 5 minutes until it is smooth. Wrap any unused dough in cling film to keep it soft.

Baking Dough

Dough models need to be baked before you can decorate them. Place them on a baking tray in the bottom of the oven at Gas Mark 1/125°C/275°F. After 30 minutes, increase to Gas Mark 3/170°C/325°F until the model is golden brown – the time will depend on the size of your model. Ask an adult to help you when using an oven.

If you see air bubbles in the dough, carefully press them with a blunt knife, and then carry on baking.

Making Shapes

You can roll and pat pieces of salt-dough or clay into any shape you want. Roll long sausages into coils, and pat balls into cubes.

Making Joins

To join two pieces of salt-dough, use some water as 'glue'. Wet the facing sides with a paintbrush dipped in water and then carefully press the pieces of dough together. You don't need much water for this.

To join self-hardening clay, use a knife to make some criss-cross marks on the surfaces to be joined. This is called *scoring*. Press the pieces gently together.

Special Effects

Press your 'clay' through a garlic press, or a sieve, to make spaghetti hair and other special effects, such as grass and trees.

Holes and Hooks

Make holes with a straw or knitting needle. Hooks can be stuck in the top of your model. Staples or paper-clips make ideal hooks.

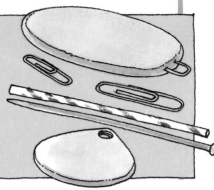

BASIC DECORATION

The decorating techniques shown here will help to make your models look really stunning. They can all be used on both self-hardening clay and salt-dough, but you will have to let your models dry out or cool down before painting them.

Impressing

Before your models harden, you can create patterns by pressing all sorts of objects against the surface.

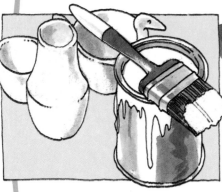

Underpainting

Paint your models with white emulsion paint to give a smooth surface for decorating.

Paintbrushes

Use large brushes to paint the background, and add details with small fine brushes.

Marbling

Using a sponge to dab a lighter colour on top of a darker base will give a marbled effect.

Scratching

Adding a top colour and scratching out a design will let the base colour show through.

Finishing

When your paints are dry, give your models at least one coat of polyurethane varnish in order to protect them.

BEADS & BADGES

You can make all kinds of jewellery using salt-dough and templates. For badges you'll need special fastenings, called *findings*, which can be bought from art-and-craft shops.

Pendants

Cut some hearts and stars from thin card. Roll out some salt-dough, and cut around the templates. Press a hook into the top of each piece. Bake, and when cool, paint and varnish. Then you can thread your pendants onto some coloured cord.

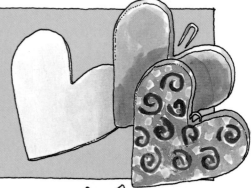

Badges

You can make some great dinosaur badges with templates, too. Stick a badge finding to the back before putting them in the oven. Then paint them any colour you like. Don't forget a coat of varnish.

Necklaces

Salt-dough is great for making beads of all shapes and sizes. Don't forget to make a hole through all of your beads. A thin knitting needle is ideal for this. You could also make some fish pendants to hang on your necklace. Follow the instructions for the other pendants (above). After you have shaped your beads, bake them and let them cool. Thread them back onto the knitting needle to make it easier to paint and varnish them. When they are dry, you can thread them onto some strong nylon thread.

A SUN PLAQUE

A relief is a design in which raised patterns or decorations are modelled onto a flat surface. That's how this sun is made – it will look great hanging on your wall. Don't forget to add a hook to the top of the plaque before you bake it.

1

Lay a small plate onto some rolled-out salt-dough, and then cut around it with a knife.

2

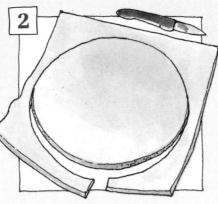

Roll out some more dough. Cut around a larger plate to make the outer circle.

3

Wet the facing edges with water and gently press the small circle onto the large one.

4

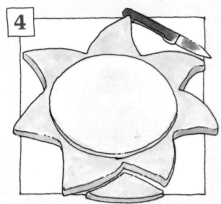

Carefully cut out the dough around the outer circle to make the seven sun rays.

5

Model a nose, mouth, eyes, and eyebrows. Stick them onto the circle. Add a hook.

6

Bake in the oven, and when your sun has cooled down, you can paint and varnish it.

Moon and Stars

These moon and star decorations can also be hung on the wall, or from the ceiling as a mobile. Make templates, roll out some dough and cut out your shapes. Add hooks and bake. Cool, paint and varnish.

DOOR DECORATIONS

Painted magnets brighten up any fridge door. Or you can use the relief technique to make a personalised doorplate for your room. You can buy small magnets from art-and-craft shops.

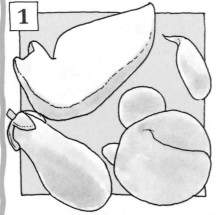

Fridge Magnets

Model the shapes from small pieces of salt-dough. Don't make them too big or they'll fall off the fridge. You can also use the relief technique (see page 12) to build up special features.

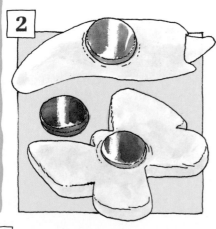

Before baking, press a small magnet into the back of each shape. Bake with the magnets facing upwards. When they have cooled down, paint the models with bright colours. Add a final coat of varnish.

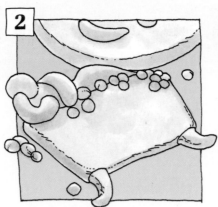

Doorplates

Roll out some dough and cut out several different shapes. You can use an upturned glass to make perfect circles.

With small pieces of dough, model the details on the bath and the face. Don't forget to add some curly hair (see page 7).

Make a hole in the top or add a hook. Bake, and when cool, paint your models. Add varnish.

The bath and ship shown here are great for any bathroom. You could hang the others on your bedroom door.

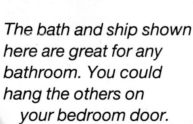

EVERLASTING FOOD

Why not make this tasty-looking plate of egg and chips for a special tea party, with fruit tarts to follow? They look good enough to eat, but make sure nobody takes a bite by mistake!

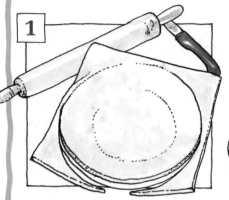

Lay some rolled-out salt-dough over a lightly greased plate. Trim the edges with a knife.

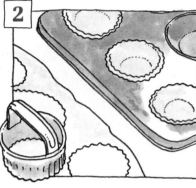

Cut out some pastry cases from a thin piece of dough. Press them into a greased bun tin.

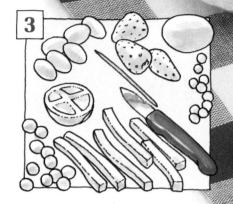

Model the chips, peas, tomato and fruit from balls of dough. The egg is made from two pieces of clay stuck together and flattened. Use a cocktail stick to mark the fruit and tomato.

Arrange the food as you want. Lift it again, and then stick it all down with a little water.

Bake, paint and varnish your models. Don't forget to decorate the plate, too!

Bake the models on the plate and in the bun tin. They will slide off when cool. Be careful though – your models can also break easily.

17

TERRIFIC TILES

You can also use the relief technique to make these colourful tiles. Make sure you choose a pattern which can be divided into four or more parts, as shown in step 1 below.

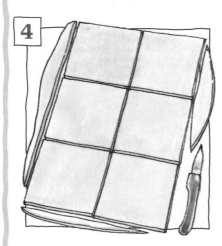

1 Divide a sheet of paper into large squares and work out your simple, repeating pattern.

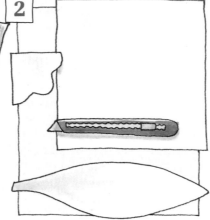

2 Make a card template, 15 x 15 cm, for the tile, and for the different shapes in your design.

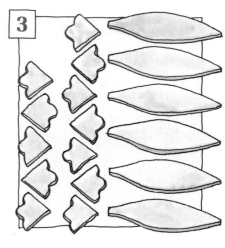

3 Roll out some salt-dough and, using your templates, cut out the small shapes.

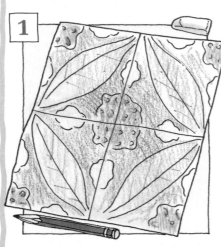

4 Roll out another piece of dough and cut out six tiles, using the large template as a guide.

5 Stick the dough shapes onto each tile with water, following your original pencil design.

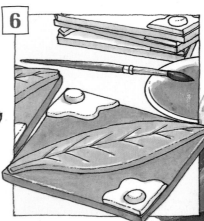

6 Bake, and when cool, paint and varnish your tiles using the same colours on each one.

When the tiles have dried, you can push them all together to make up your original pattern. You can get some great ideas for further designs and colours from catalogues produced by different tile suppliers.

19

MERRY MERMAID

Once you've mastered badges, you can go on to something bigger – a complete picture! The one shown here has an underwater theme, but you can create any scene – maybe set in outer space, or in a deep, dark jungle.

1

Roll out a piece of dough to about 1 cm thick. From this, cut out a rectangle 22 x 16 cm. This will be the base of your underwater picture.

2

Using just a little water, wet and then stick thin sausages around the edge of your picture to make a wavy border. Smooth the join.

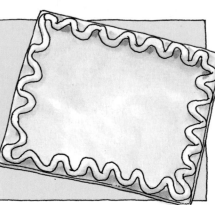

3

Shape a head for the mermaid and add some hair. Then make an oval body, some arms and a tail. Wet and stick everything onto your picture.

4 Cut a vest out of some thin dough and use it to cover the joins of the body and arms. Use a paperclip to impress the scales onto the fishy tail.

5 Make some small fish, starfish and shells using card templates. Stick everything onto your picture with water. You can also add a hook if you want to hang the picture up.

6 Now bake your picture and when it has cooled down, paint it with bright colours. Add some gold or silver paint to the border and also to the tail to make shimmering scales. Then finish off with a coat of varnish.

DANCER & CLOWN

These colourful figures are made from salt-dough, with spaghetti hair and bright costumes. They are modelled directly onto a baking sheet and are made to be hung up. To make free-standing figures, see More Ideas (page 40).

1 Small balls of dough make the heads, and larger oval shapes make the bodies.

2 Use a single sausage to make the arms and two thicker sausages to form the legs.

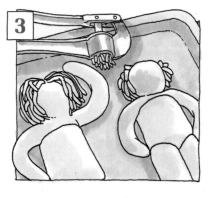

3 Make some curly hair for your figures, (see page 7), and stick it on with a little water.

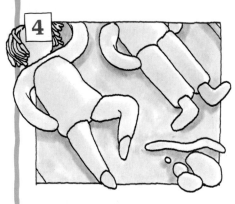

4 Use small pieces of dough for the feet. Make a pair of small pointed ones for the dancer, and some big flat feet for the clown. Stick them to the end of the legs.

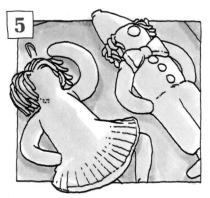

5 Add a nose, a bow tie, a pointed clown's hat, and buttons. Cover the joins with baggy trousers and a pretty ballet dress. Don't forget to add a hook to each model.

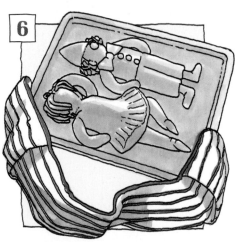

6 Bake your models. When they have cooled down, paint them with bright colours. Add a coat of varnish.

BOWLS & POTS

This is the first of several activities using self-hardening clay. The clay is soft and easy to work with, but dries really hard. You can make pots in any size, but don't put any water in them – they're not waterproof!

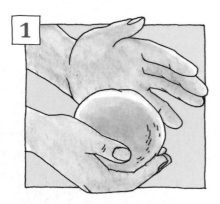

1 Roll a large ball of clay in the palm of your hand until it is smooth and even all over.

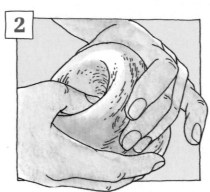

2 Press your thumb in the middle of the clay, and keep turning the ball until it forms a bowl.

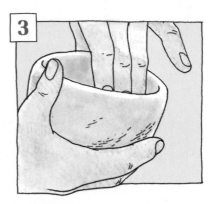

3 Hold the clay in one hand, and use the other to gently pinch out the sides of the bowl.

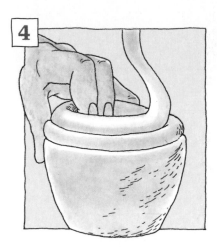

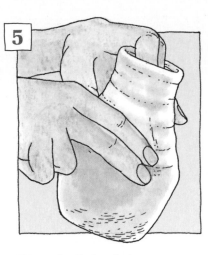

To make a tall pot, roll some thick sausages and coil them around to build up the neck.

Blend all the joins together, and smooth down the pot, both inside and out.

Decorate one bowl by adding a bird's head to one side of the rim, and a tail to the other.

When the clay is dry, you can paint and decorate your pots with bright colours. When the paint is dry, add a final coat of polyurethane varnish.

ALL SORTS OF BOXES

A pretty box would make an ideal birthday or Christmas present for a friend, or you could keep it for yourself and use it to keep all your bits and pieces in.

1
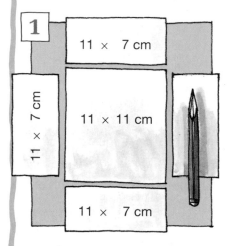

Cut out five card templates – one for the base and two for each side, as shown.

2
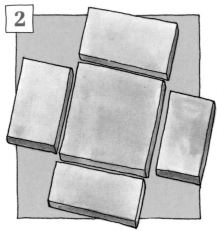

Roll out some clay to about 1 cm thick. Cut out one base piece and four side pieces.

3
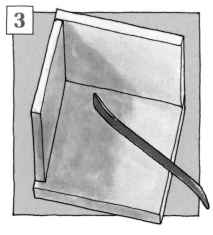

Join the sides to the base by scoring and blending the edges together (see page 7).

4
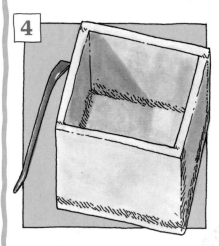

Use a modelling tool and your fingers to blend and smooth down all of the joins and surfaces.

5

The lid is the same size as your base. Score and stick a square, 9 x 9 cm, in the middle.

6

Turn the lid over and add a handle. Let the clay dry completely before you decorate your box.

Boxes Galore!

You can go on to make lots of other boxes in different sizes and shapes. Just follow the basic technique of using card templates and some rolled-out clay. Why not have a go at making either a triangular or a rectangular box? You could even try making a hexagonal one!

CYLINDERS & RINGS

Once you've learned the basic technique for making cylinders, you can adapt it to make all sorts of things. Try this pencil holder and the napkin rings for starters.

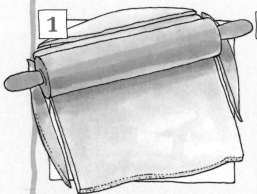

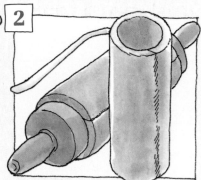

Cylinder Pots

1. Roll out and cut a clay rectangle. Wrap it loosely round the pin.

2. Ease the tube off, then blend the two edges back together.

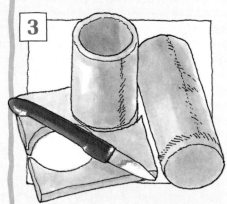

3. Roll out some more clay to the same thickness. Carefully cut around the cylinder to make the round base.

4. Join the cylinder to the base and smooth the join. When the pot is dry, decorate and varnish it.

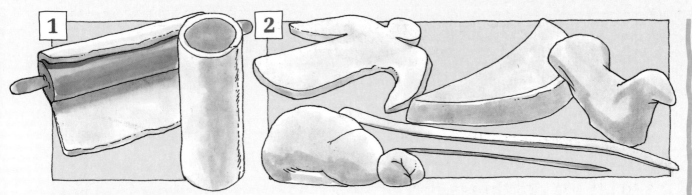

Napkin Rings

Following steps 1-2 on page 28, make a large clay cylinder.

Roll out some more clay and cut out angels with wings. Cut some crescents to make birds. Shape one end into a bird's tail, and the other into a head.

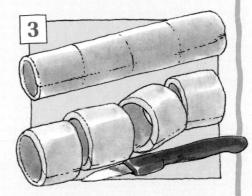

Carefully cut your large cylinder into smaller rings as shown.

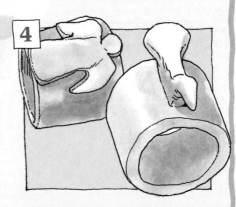

Score and press the angels and birds onto the rings. When dry, brightly paint and varnish them.

AN EGYPTIAN BOAT

This idea comes from a model boat found in an Ancient Egyptian tomb. If you look in history books and museums, you'll be able to find all sorts of ideas – people have been making models for hundreds of years.

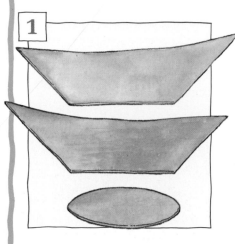

1

Draw and cut out some card templates for the sides and bottom of your boat. You can make them any size you like, but put the templates together before you use the clay.

When you are happy that they all fit together properly, roll out some self-hardening clay to about 1 cm thick. Carefully cut around your card templates with a knife.

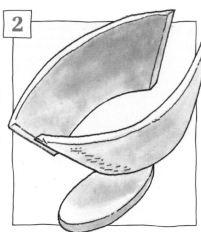

2

Score the clay and then gently bend the side pieces to fit onto the base. Pinch the ends of the two sides together. Smooth the joins.

Cut out a small clay crosspiece for the inside of the boat. Roll out another piece of clay for the deck and lay it on the boat. Trim the clay, score and smooth the joins. Shape the stern and add a prow.

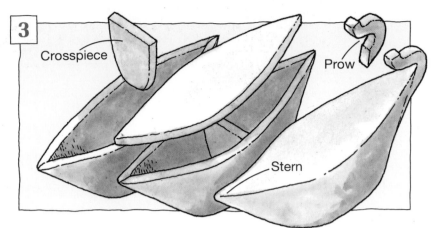

Crosspiece

Prow

Stern

Push cocktail sticks into the deck for canopy supports. Press some clay where the sticks go through the deck. Now add a cut-out canopy.

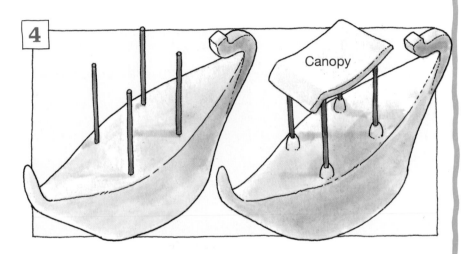

Canopy

Stick all your models onto your boat and then paint with bright colours. Add a coat of varnish.

Model some Egyptian figures, baskets and pots. Make oars by pressing small pieces of clay onto the end of cocktail sticks.

The square box technique (see page 26) can also be used to make simple houses out of self-hardening clay. The ones shown here are part of a colourful Mexican village. Perhaps you could also build a clay model of your own town or village?

House

Make a square box following steps 1-4 on page 26. For the roof, cut some clay the same size as your base, score and stick it to the top of your box. Cut out some windows and a doorway, and add a chimney. Paint your model when the clay is dry.

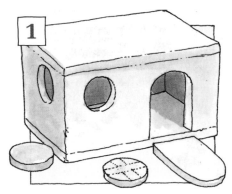  

Barn

Make a rectangular box and add a roof. Cut out an arched doorway and two round windows.

Cut crosses out of the window circles. Score and stick them back into the window spaces.

When the clay is dry, paint and varnish it.

Cactus

Complete the scene by modelling some cactus plants. Mark the clay with the end of a cocktail stick to give the cacti a prickly look.

ANIMAL FUN

Once you've learnt the basic modelling techniques, you can let your imagination run riot! You can make your own zoo, full of wild and exotic animals. Or perhaps create a farmyard, full of cows, sheep and pigs.

The animals shown here are made from pinch pots (see page 24) and cylinders (see page 28). Lay your models upside down when you add the legs. Let the clay dry completely before turning them the right way up to paint.

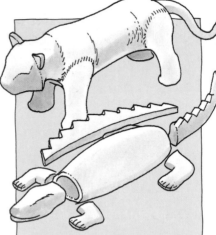

Pig

You'll need two round pinch pots (see page 24). Try to make them the same size. Score and join them together. Smooth the join.

Roll some sausages to make the legs. Score and join them to the body. Shape the head, and add some ears, a nose and a wiggly tail!

Other Animals

The lizard and tiger are easy to make from clay cylinders (see page 28). The head, legs and tail are shaped from clay and joined to the pot. Then you just need to paint on any special markings they have.

MARVELLOUS MASKS

Many ancient cultures used colourful masks to decorate their homes. You can make these cheerful masks to hang on your own bedroom wall.

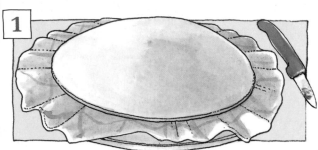

1

Put a tea towel over an upside-down plate. Lay a piece of clay on the plate and trim away the edges.

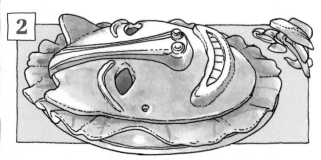

2

Cut out the eyes, then use the relief method (see page 12) to add the nose, eyebrows, ears and mouth.

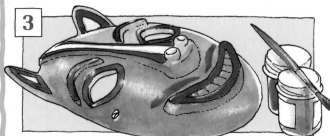

3

Make two holes or add a hook. When dry, paint and varnish your mask.

These masks are too heavy to be worn, but you can thread some ribbon or wire through the holes to hang them on your wall. Once you have mastered the technique of making masks, you can adapt it to make all sorts of faces. You could make animal masks, adding pipe cleaners or straws for whiskers.

37

A FISH PLAQUE

You can also use plaster of Paris to make models (buy it at an art-and-craft shop). You'll need a soft material such as modelling clay to make a mould for your models.

1

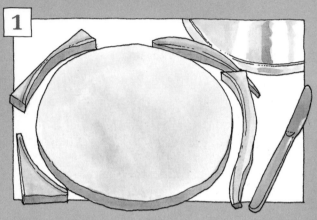

To make the round base, first roll out a large piece of soft clay. It needs to be about 2 cm thick. Then cut around a plate or bowl with a modelling knife.

2

Use a modelling tool to carve out a fish and a starfish. Impress the scales (see page 8) with a paperclip. Use shells to impress a border pattern.

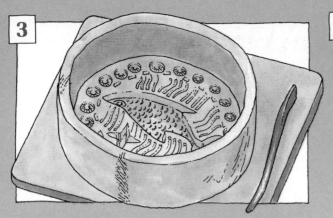

Roll out another thick piece of soft clay, about 4 cm deep and long enough to fit around the base. Score and press it firmly onto the base.

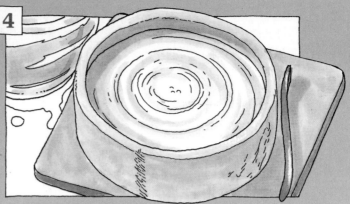

Following the instructions, mix the plaster in a plastic bowl and carefully pour it into the mould. Don't fill the mould completely to the top.

When the plaster has set really hard, gently pull away the clay. Smooth any rough edges and then paint and varnish your plaque.

MORE IDEAS

You can make your own printing blocks from self-hardening clay. Either carve or use the relief method to make your design. When the clay has dried, dip the blocks in paint and use them to decorate your own wrapping paper or notepaper.

Some modelling 'clays' stay soft and come in lots of colours. These make great dinosaurs and other animals.

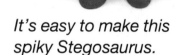

It's easy to make this spiky Stegosaurus.

Try making free-standing figures using a support. Glass bottles are ideal. Wrap some clay around the bottle and then build your model. The bottle lets the model stand up.